AF264486

Flower Loom in Bloom

Beginners Guide
to
Making Flowers

Ashli Couch and Theresa Jewell

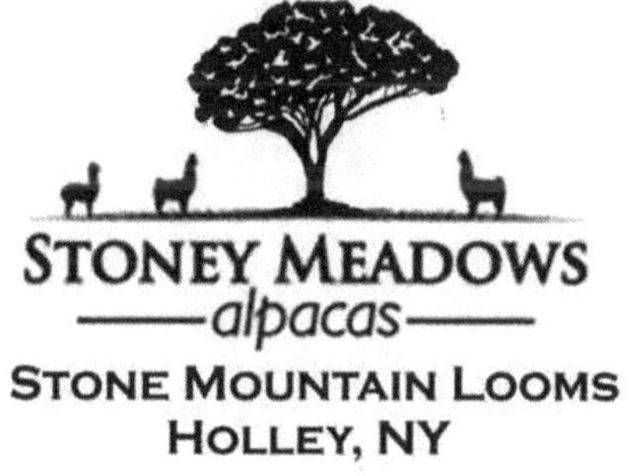

STONE MOUNTAIN LOOMS
HOLLEY, NY

How to Make a

Flower

on the

Flower Loom

Make Large Pedals

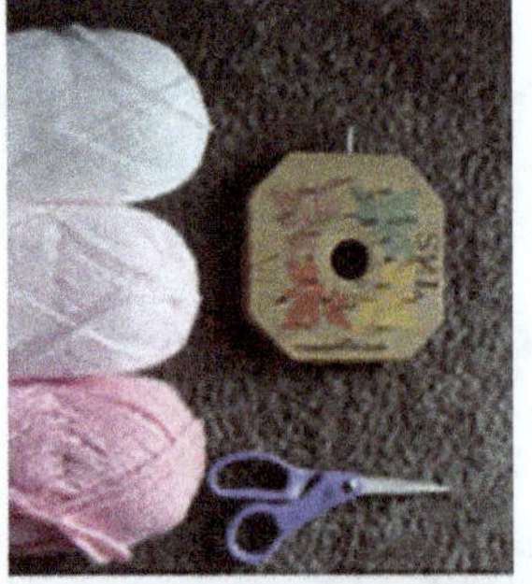

Step 1: Start with the color yarn you'd like to be the big 'pedals' by dropping the yarn through the center of your loom. Make a slip knot and secure it to the nail located on the edge of your loom. This is so you can pull and tug on your working yarn without fear of pulling to hard and having to start over again.

Suggestion: Don't make the slip knot really tight. It's ok if it's a little loose and may come in handy later.

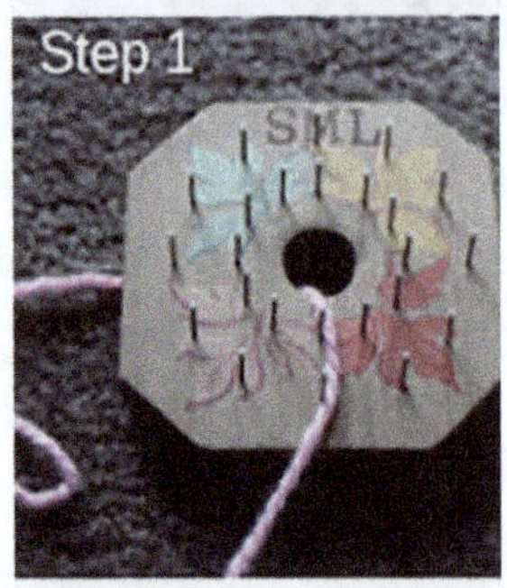

Step 2: Now you're ready to begin making your flower. Start by picking an outside nail to start on. We suggest you start on the nail opposite from the nail you just secured your slip knot to. You're going to take your yarn to the left side of the nail and wrap around it going clockwise.

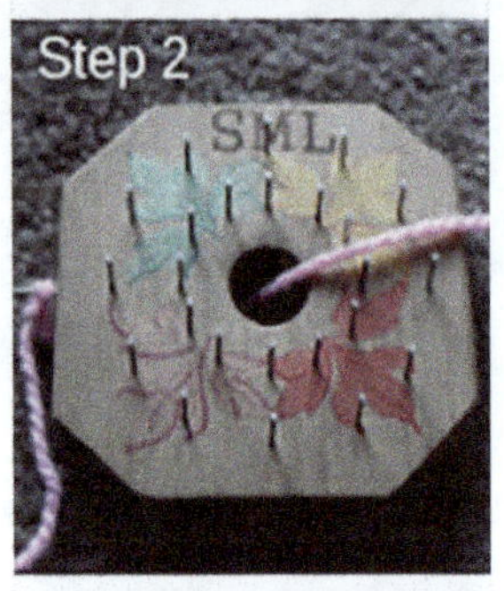

Step 3: Bring your yarn straight down to the opposite nail. This time you'll be on the right side of the nail, but you will still wrap the yarn clockwise around the nail.

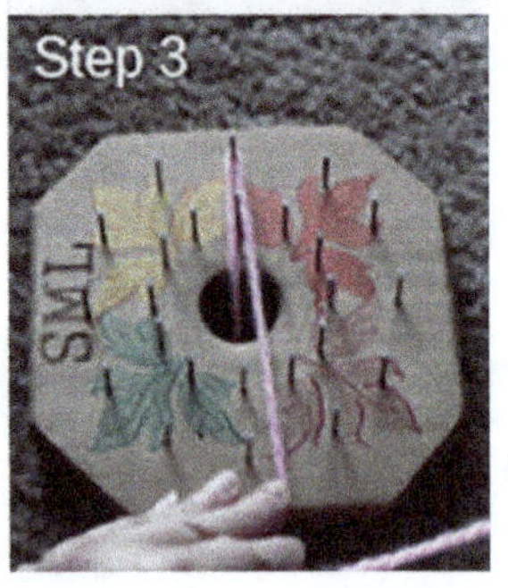

Step 4: Take your yarn back across the center. This time you are going to wrap your yarn, still clockwise, around the nail to the right of the last nail you wrapped your yarn around.

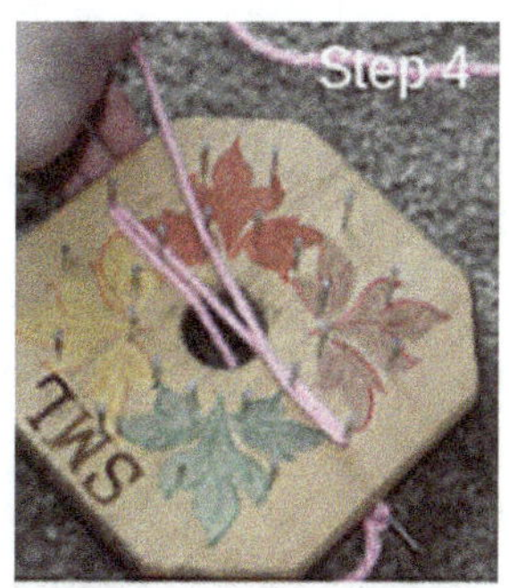

Step 5: Bring your yarn straight down and once again wrap it around the nail to the left of the last night you used.

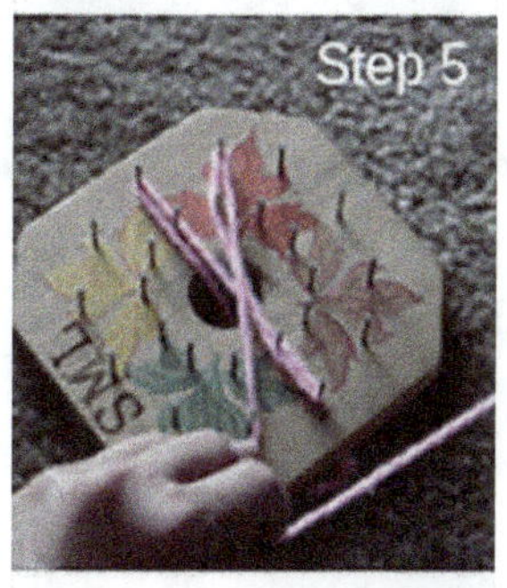

Step 6: Repeat steps 2 to 5 until you have wrapped 2 'pedals' around each nail. *You can do one 'pedal' if you want or even 3. Play around with how many pedals you'd like. Ashli prefers 2, while Theresa prefers 3, sometimes 4!

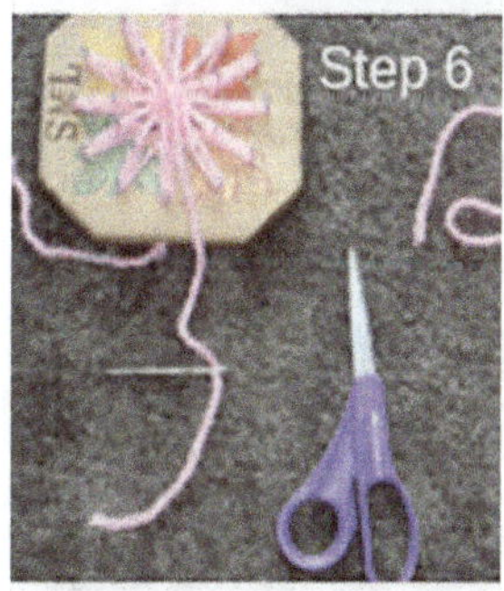

Step 7: When you are on the last nail, cut your yarn. With a tapestry needle, bring the end of the yarn through the center.

Step 8: Remove your slip knot from the nail and tie the two ends together. *If you cannot get your slip knot off, you can always cut the yarn as close to the slip knot as possible so you still have enough yarn to tie a knot with.

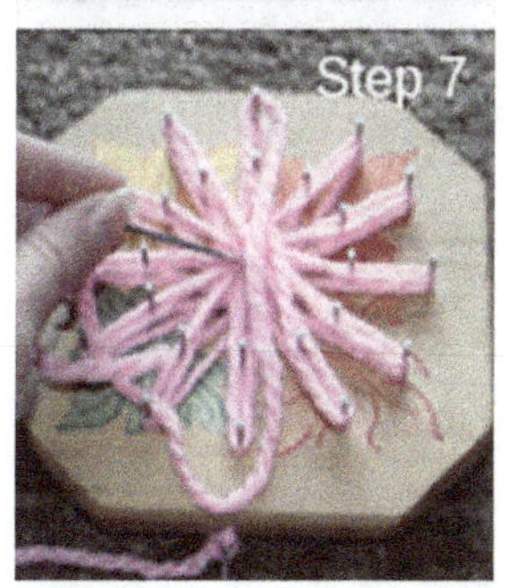

Make Small Pedals

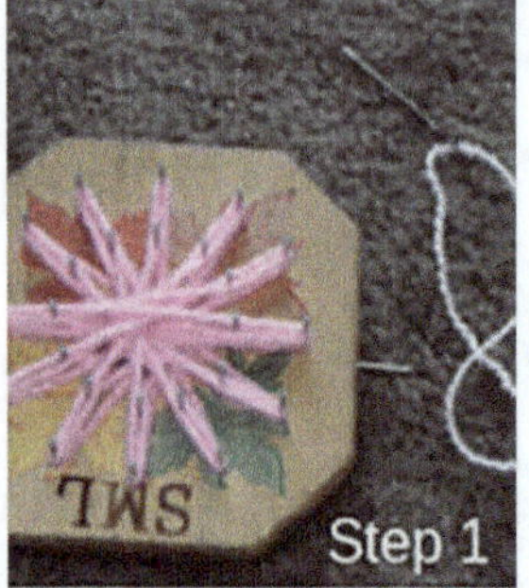

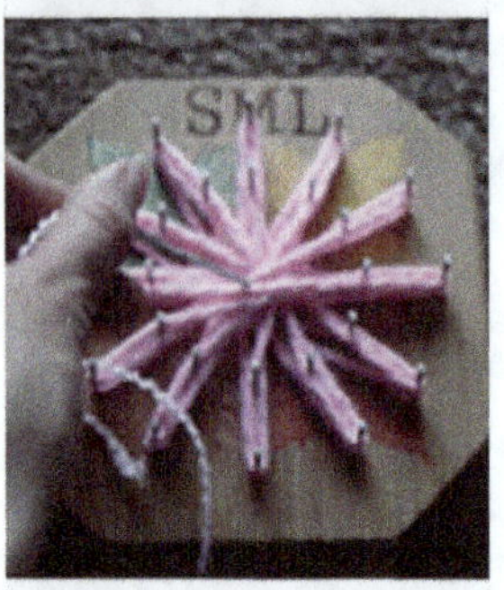

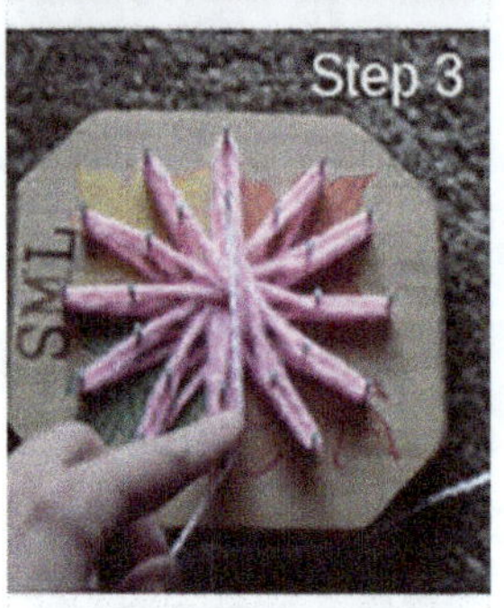

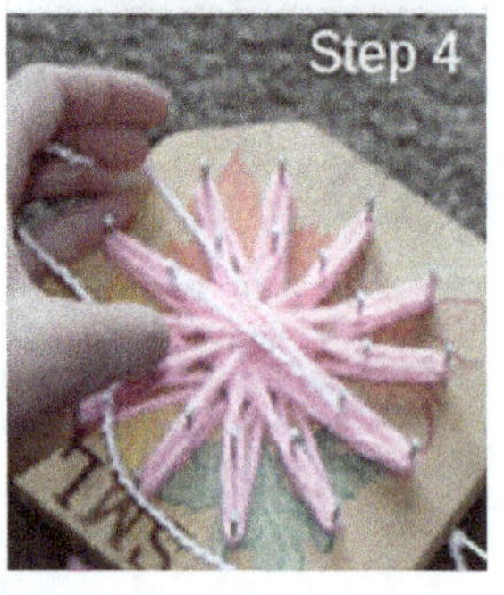

Now that you have your large pedals made, it is time to make some smaller pedals. *Again this is entirely up to you. You can skip ahead to Finishing your Flower if you'd like to just leave it as is, or you can add more pedals.

Step 1: I personally like to change up my color yarn, but you do not have to. If you'd like to keep going with the first color then do not cut your yarn and tie it yet. You can keep going. If you are changing colors, then thread your new color yarn on a tapestry needle and bring your yarn through the center.

Step 2: Create a slip knot and once again put it on the nail on the outside. *I still suggest a loose slip knot.

Step 3: Let's start our small pedals. I suggest you use the same nail to start on as you started your large pedals. Bring your yarn to the left side and wrap around going clockwise. This time you are wrapping around the nail closer to the center.

Step 4: Bring the yarn straight down, like you did with the large pedals, and wrap around the nail closer to the center.

Step 5: Bring your yarn up to the nail on the right of your first nail and wrap around clockwise.

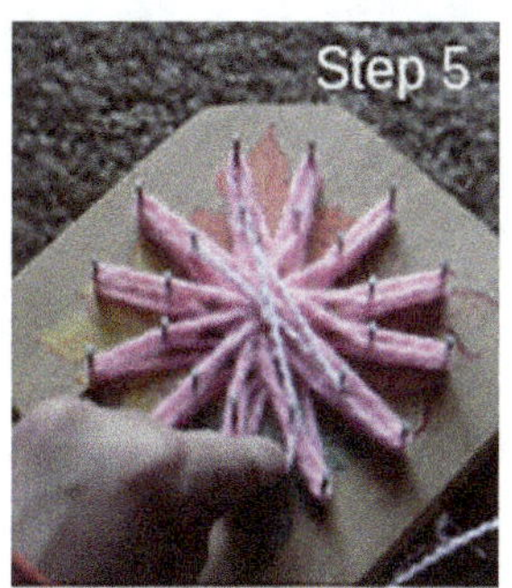

Step 6: Repeat steps 3-5 until you have wrapped 2 small pedals around the nails closets to the center. *Again you can do 1 or more pedals, it is up to you. I just like being consistent with 2 large and 2 small.

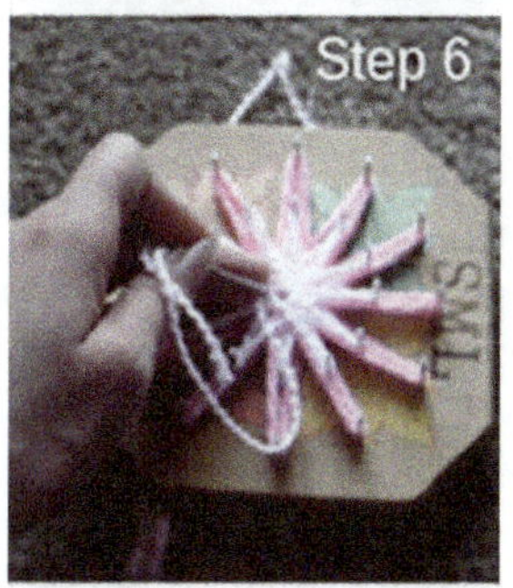

Step 7: Cut your yarn, thread the end with a tapestry needle and bring the yarn through the center. Take your slip knot off the side nail and tie the two ends together.

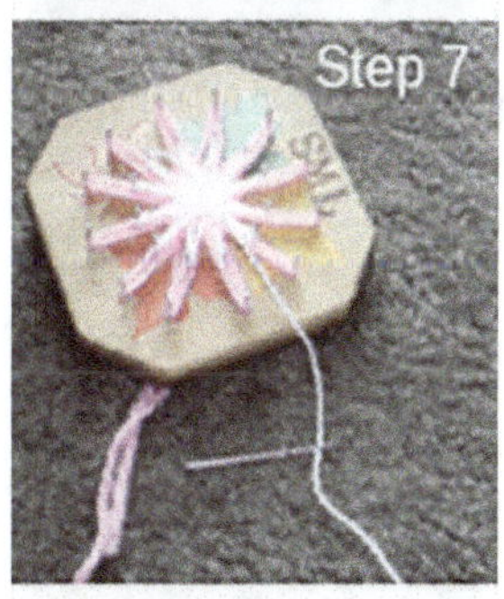

***

There are a few different ways to finish off your flower. I am going to show you my favorite way and Theresa's favorite.

Theresa's Favorite way to finish is easier than my favorite way, so I suggest starting with this finish first.

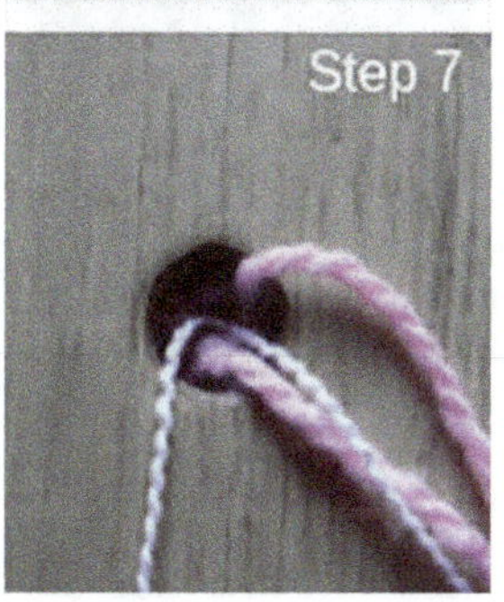

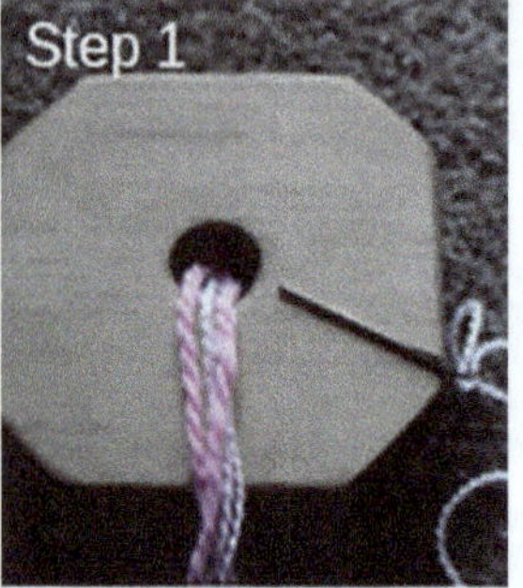

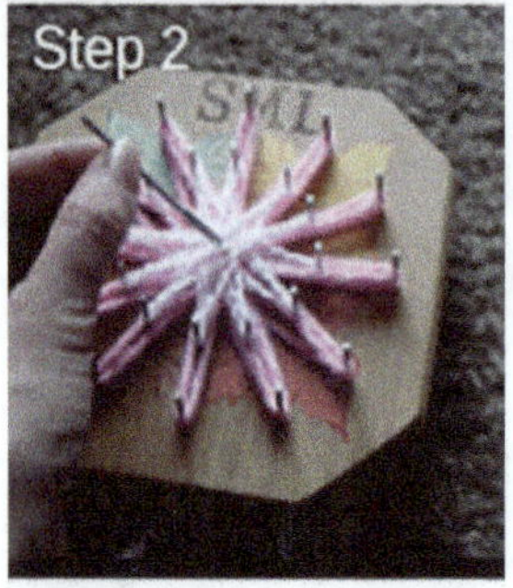

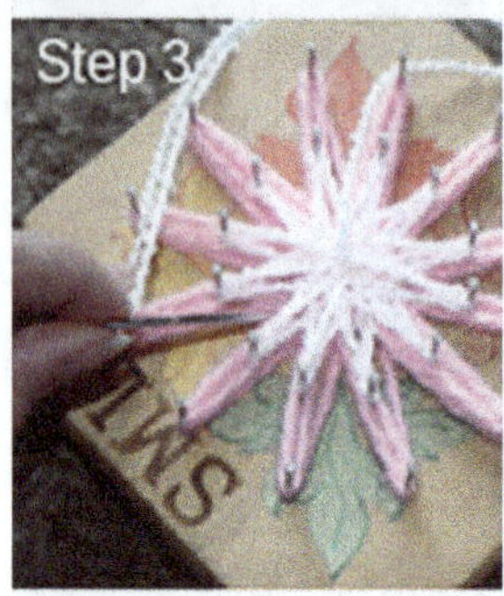

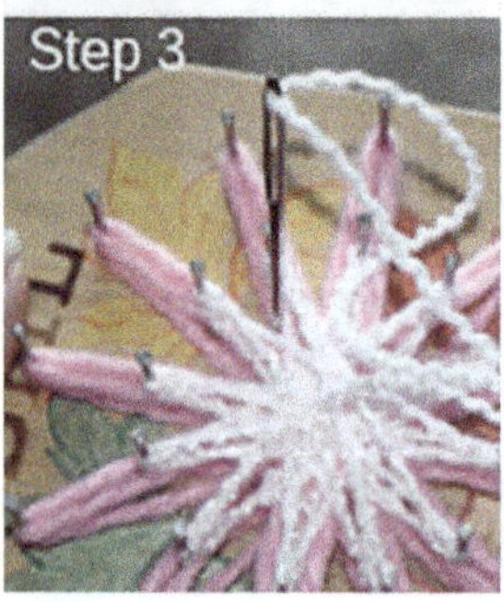

Theresa's Favorite Finish

Step 1: Pick whatever color yarn you'd like your center to be. I'm going with the same color as my larger pedals. Cut about 14"-16", or more if you feel like that will not be enough. Thread the yarn on your tapestry needle. Make a slip knot and secure it to the side nail.

Step 2: Coming from underneath the loom, bring your tapestry needle with your yarn on it up through the center.

Step 3: Pick a starting point on your loom. Working clockwise, you will fill in the center of your flower. Bring your tapestry needle in-between two nails, making sure you are on the outside of all your yarn 'pedals', pull your tapestry needle through the bottom.

Step 4: Repeat. Bring your yarn through the center, moving to the right of the last set of nails you did, sew in-between the nails/pedals. Repeat until you reach your beginning.

Step 5: Slip your slip knot off the nail (or cut it free) and tie that strand to your ending strand.

Step 6: Remove flower from the loom and enjoy! You can sew in all your ends, or leave them to use to sew the flower to another project.

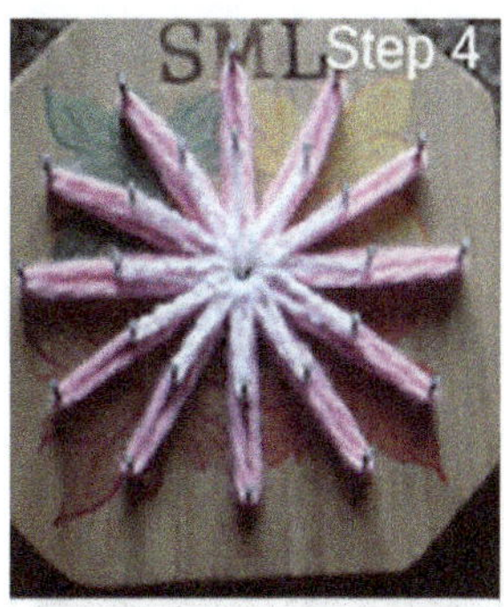

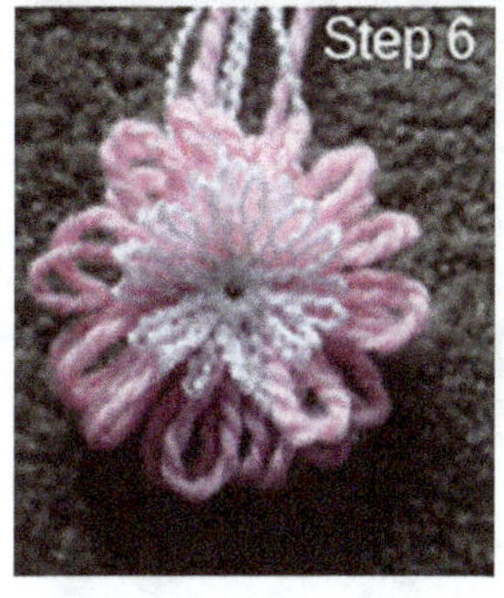

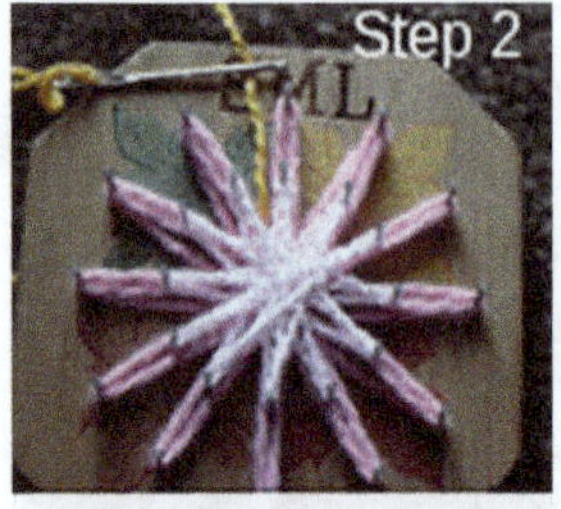

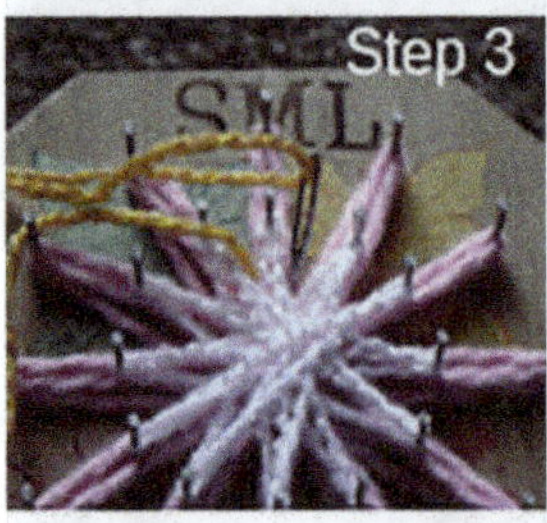

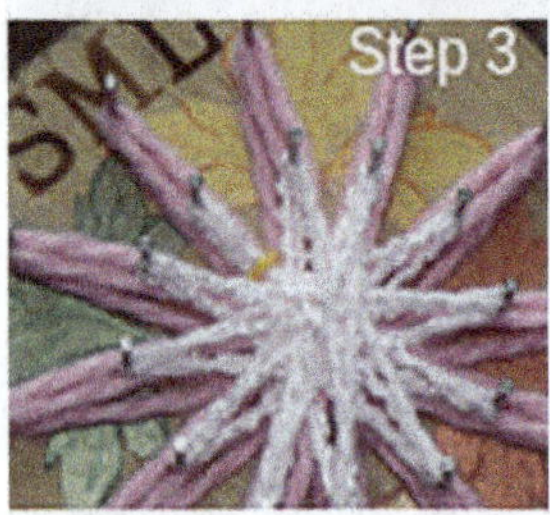

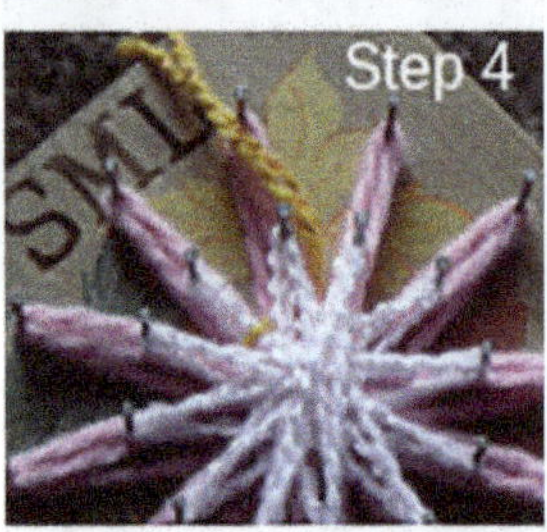

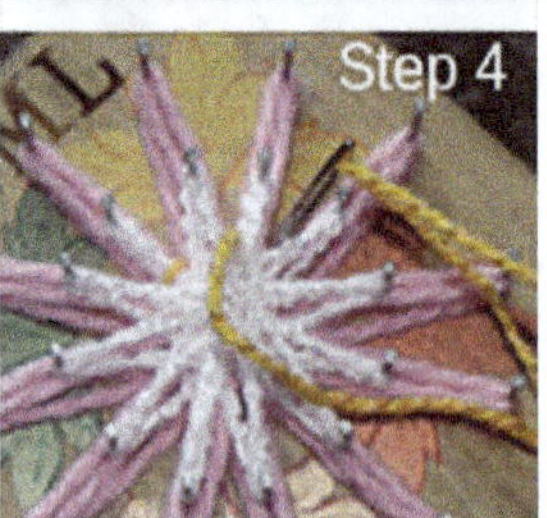

Ashli's Favorite Finish

Step 1: Pick whatever color yarn you'd like your center to be. Cut about 14"-16", or more if you feel like that will not be enough. Thread the yarn on your tapestry needle. Make a slip knot and secure it to the side nail.

Step 2: Start by coming from the back of the loom. Go in-between two of your pedals. Pull your yarn all the way through.

Step 3: Sew down in-between the next two pedals on the right. It should look like the picture with a single piece of yarn over the pedals.

Step 4: Do it again. More over one pedal, pulling your needle up from the back and then down over the next pedal. *YES you skipped a pedal! Do not worry about it, we will take care of it later.

Step 5: Repeat step 2-4 all the way around until you get to where you started sewing. You're going to sew from the back to the front where you first started. Instead of going right again, you're going to reverse it and go left, filling in the pedals you skipped earlier.

Step 6: Almost there! If you stop now, your flower will fall apart. We still haven't secured all the pedals. We are going to fix that. Now that you are back to where you began, instead of bringing your needle up in-between the pedals, you are going to bring your needle up in the center of the pedal.

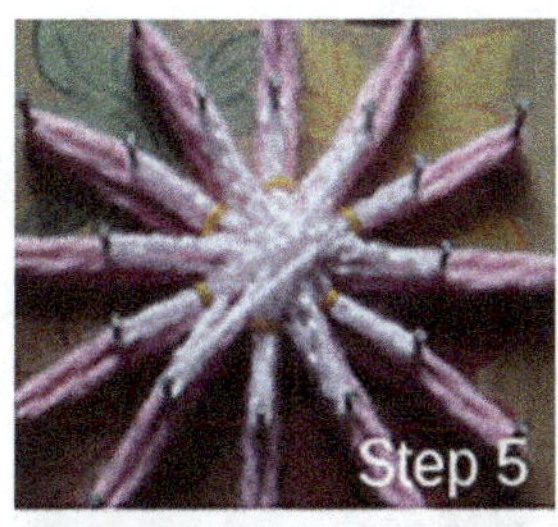

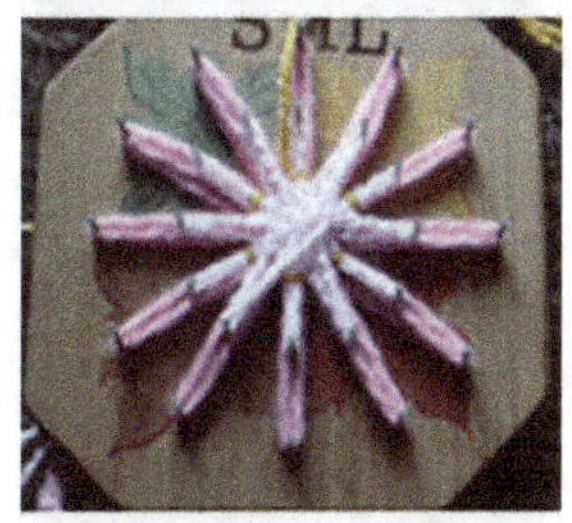

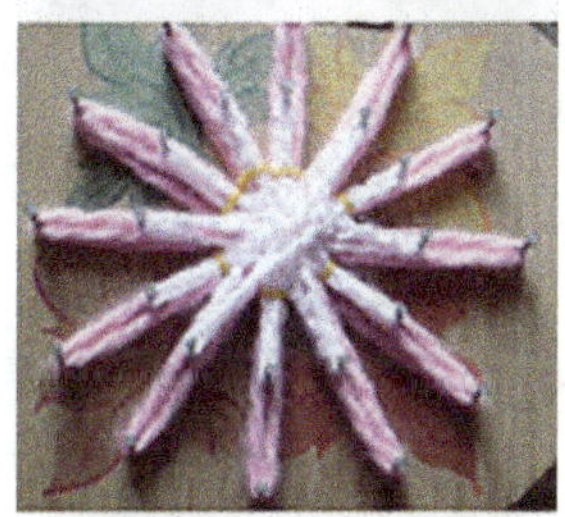

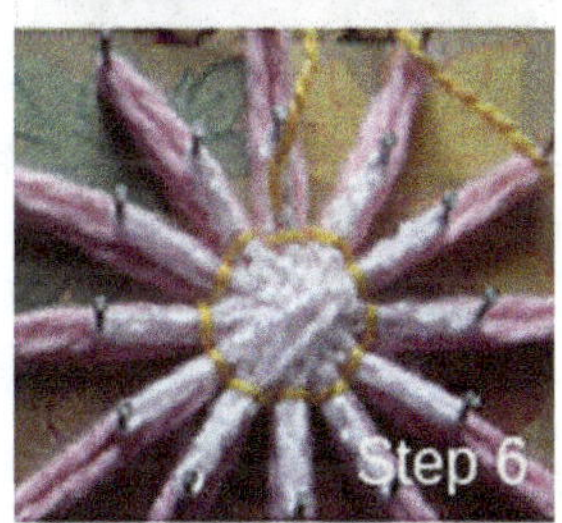

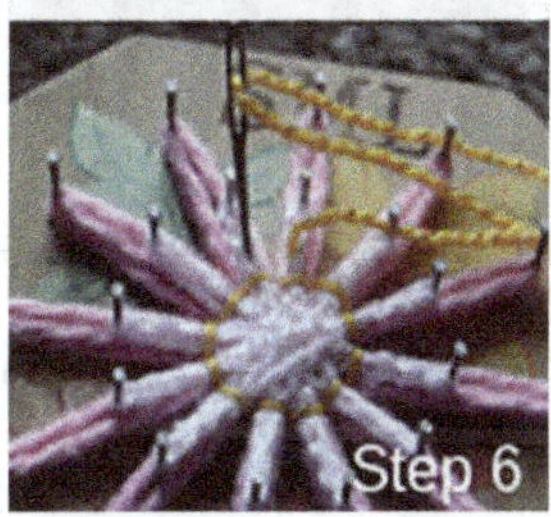

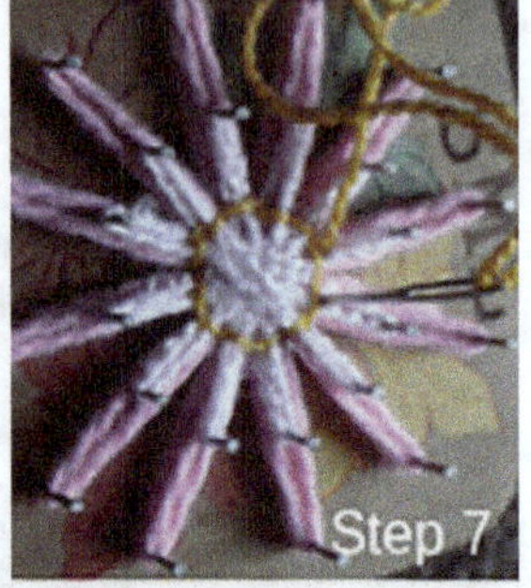

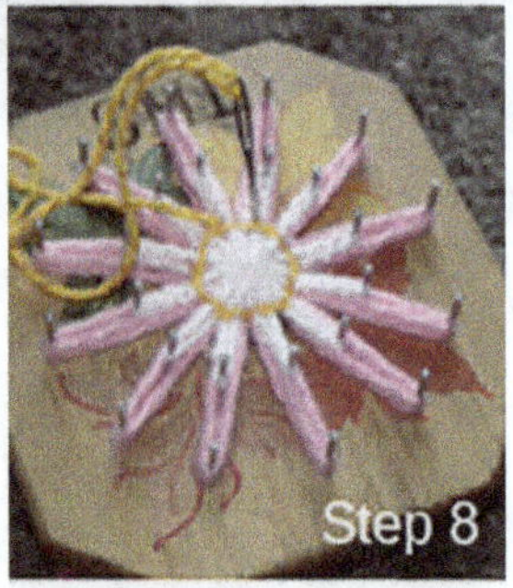

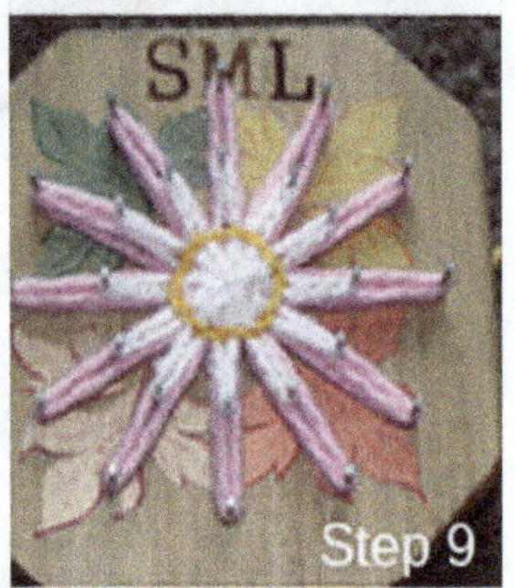

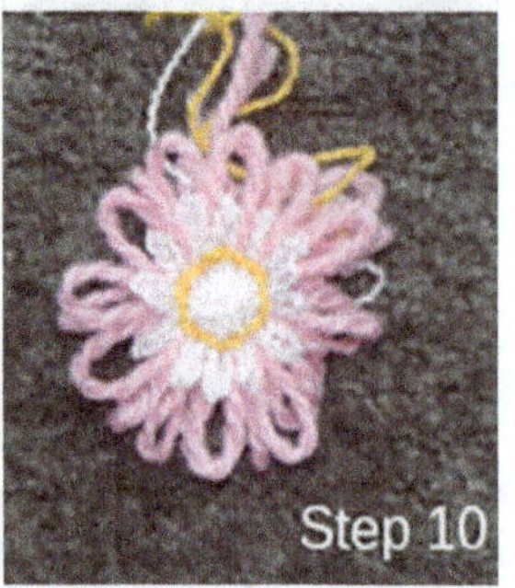

Step 7: Since you were going left, you can continue to go left around the flower. Sew in the middle of the pedals

Step 8: Keep sewing in the middle of the pedals until you reach the beginning. As you did before, you are going to reverse it and go to the right now, filling in all the pedals you skipped.

Step 9: Once you return to the beginning, do not bring your needle back up. Leave it on the back side. Flip your loom over, pull your slip knot off the nail and tie the two ends together.

Step 10: All that is left is for you to carefully slide your pedals up and off the nails, pulling your pretty flower off the loom! You can sew in all your ends, or leave them to use to sew the flower to another project.

Flower
Ideas

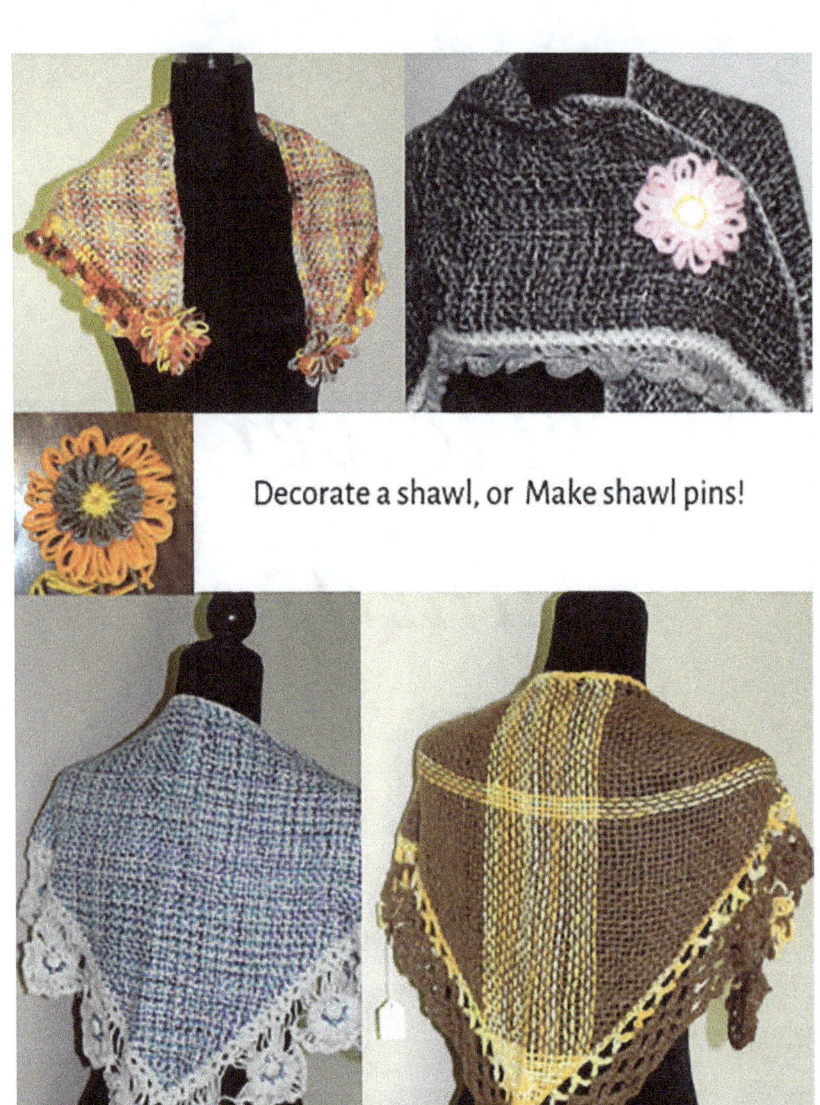

Decorate a shawl, or Make shawl pins!

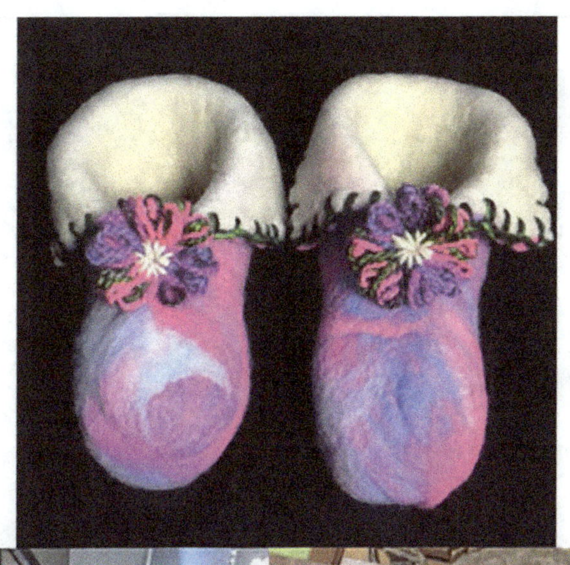

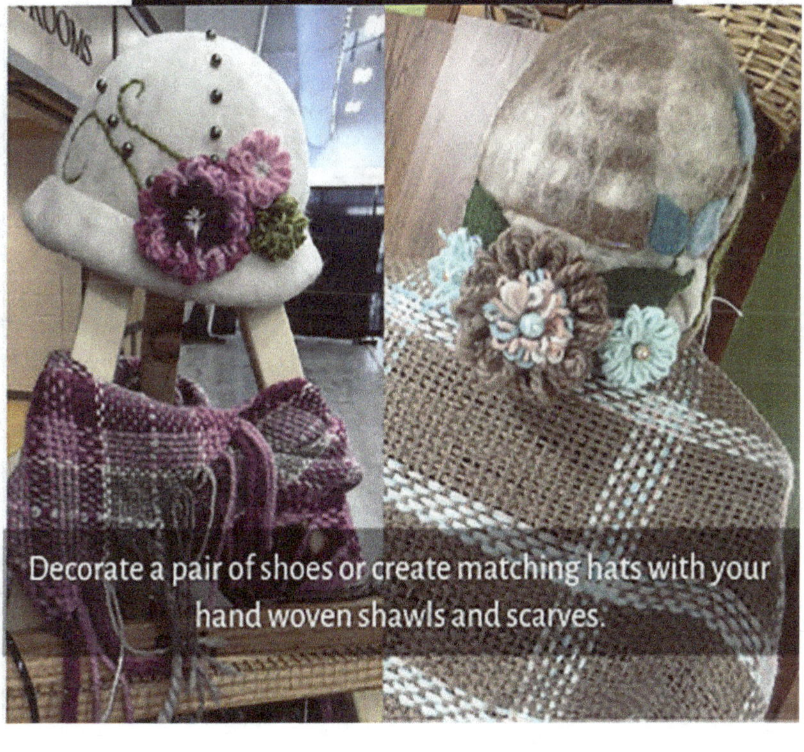

Decorate a pair of shoes or create matching hats with your hand woven shawls and scarves.

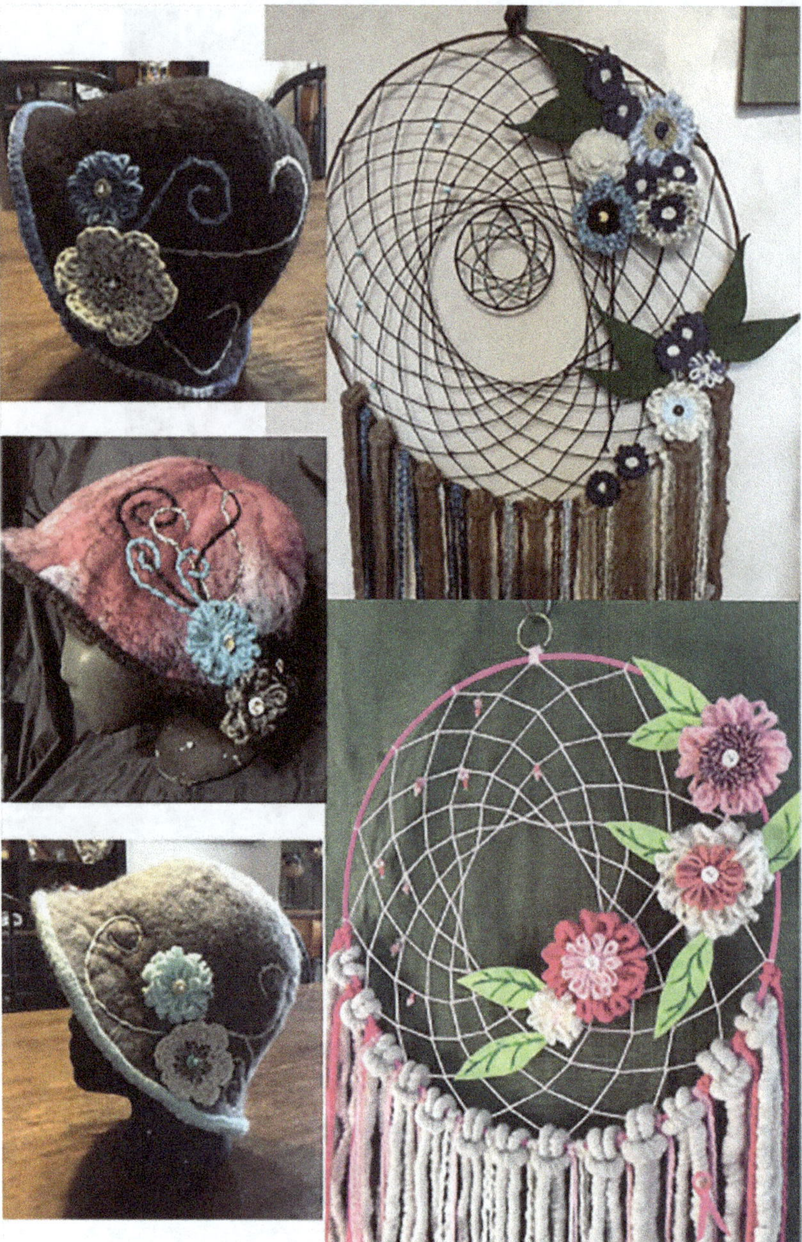

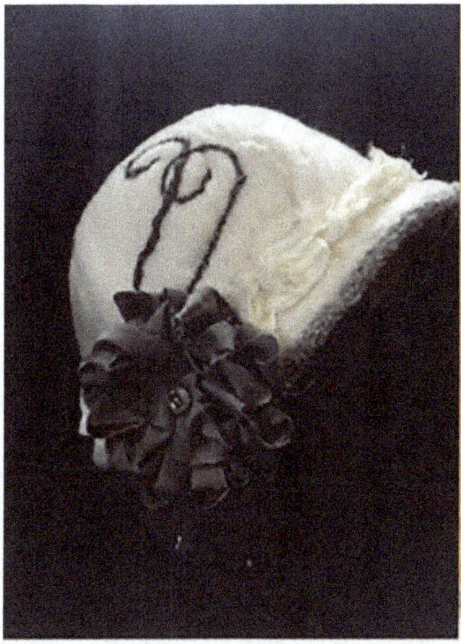

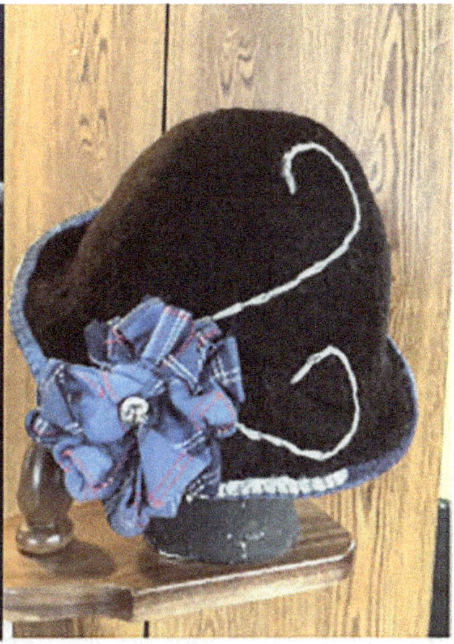

Make flowers out of stripes of fabric!
Or add a bead, a button, or even a pendant in the center.

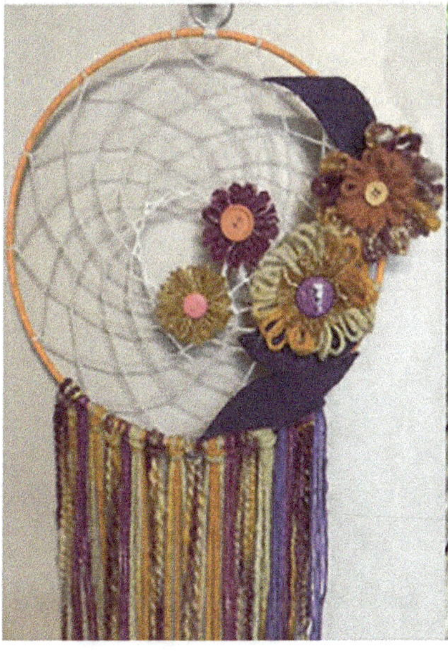

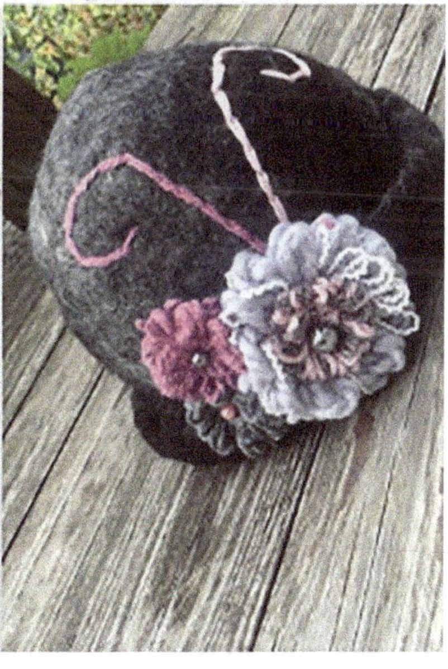

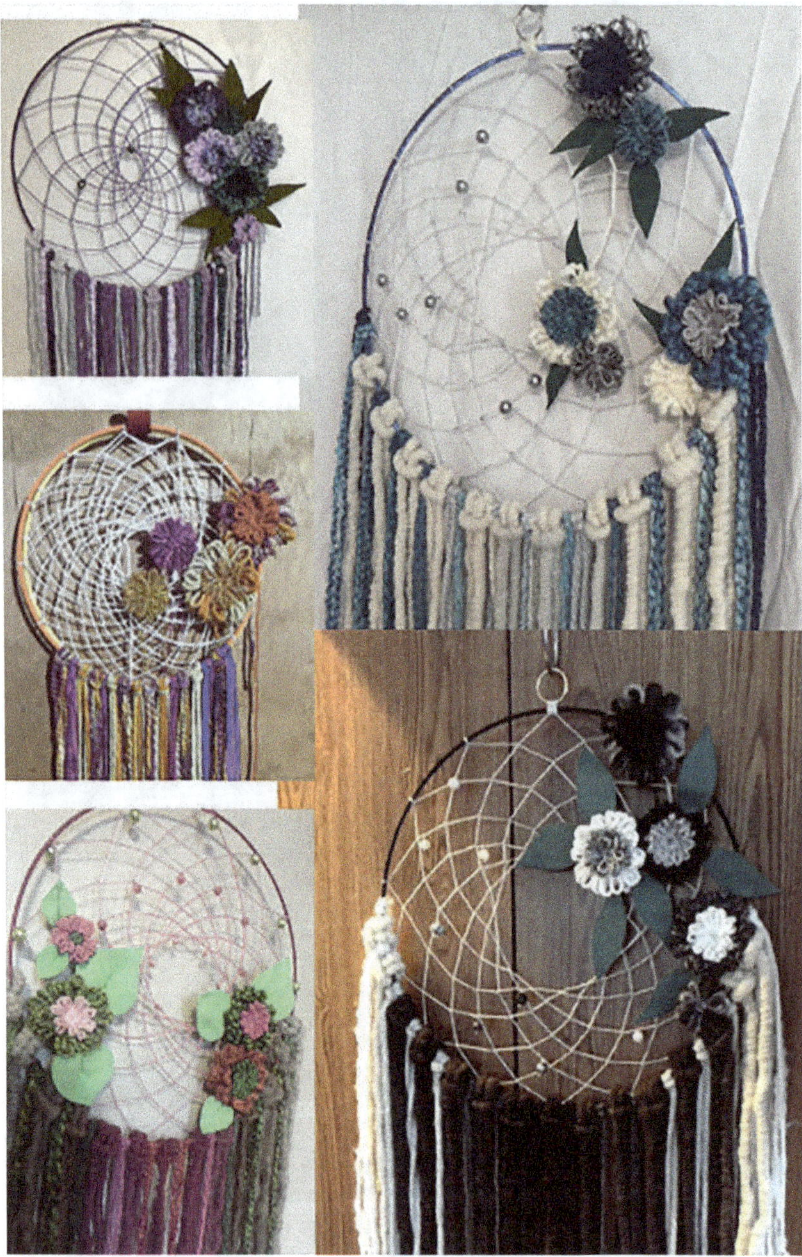

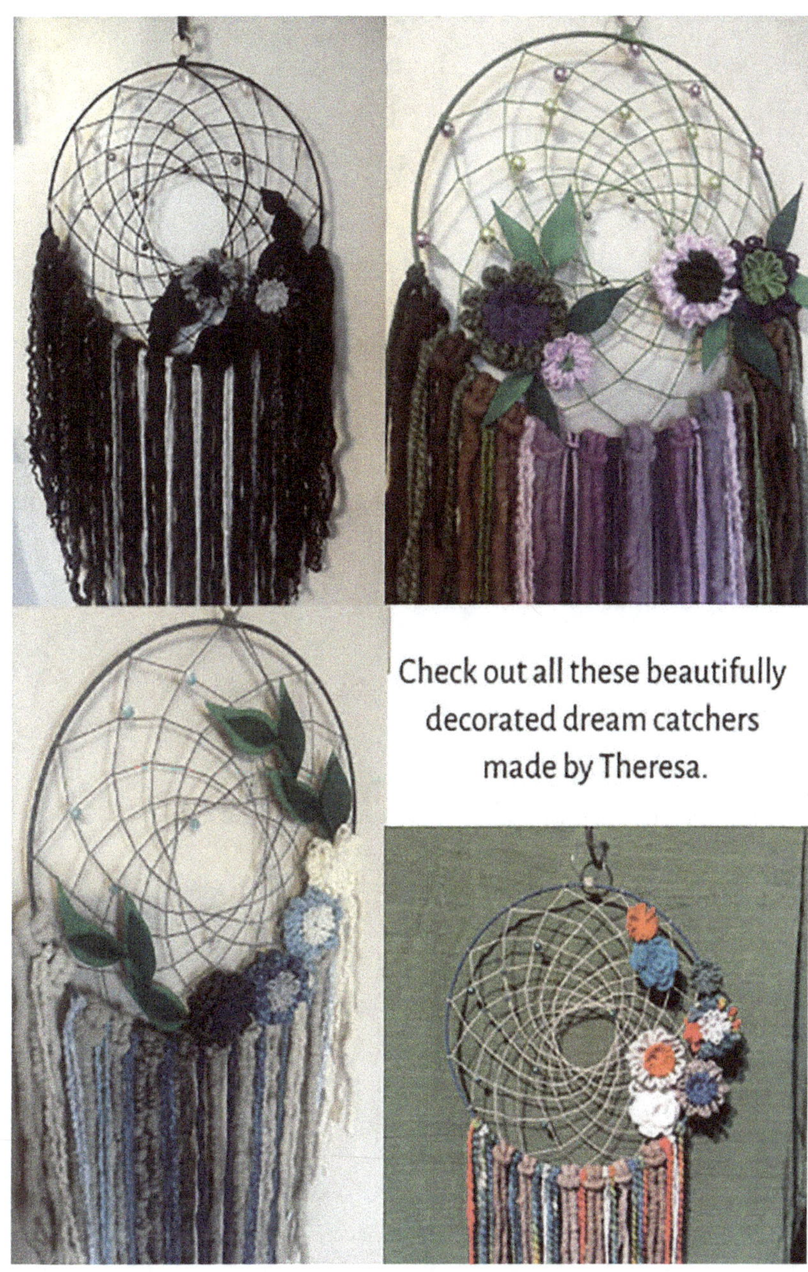

Check out all these beautifully
decorated dream catchers
made by Theresa.

Meet the Authors

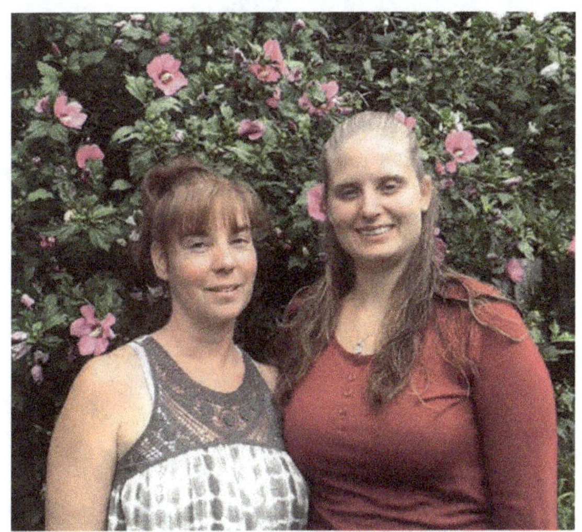

Ashli Couch (Right)

Owner of Bubbles 'n Stitches, her own little crafting business where she makes and sells all natural soaps and lotions along with all her woven and knitted items.

Ashli is self-taught in hand knitting (2011), machine knitting (2018) all natural soaps (2014), lotions (2015), yarn dying (2017), and felting (2017). She learned spinning (2012), frame loom weaving (2012), and peg loom weaving (2017) from Theresa.

Most days you can find Ashli loading up on tea, knitting, weaving, making soap, appeasing her kitties, and working hard on the next weaving book with Theresa.

Theresa Jewell (Left)

Co-Owner of Stone Mountain Looms and Stoney Meadows Alpacas Farm with her husband Chuck Jewell.

Theresa is a self-taught yarn artist and has continued to learn and inspire others. Her knowledge of yarn crafts includes: spinning (2002), yarn dying (2002), frame loom weaving (2003), peg loom weaving (2009), tapestry loom weaving (2017), crochet, and felting.

Most days you can find Theresa at her farm taking care of her 'yarn babies' aka her alpaca and sheep or playing with yarn and coming up with more patterns to share in the next book. She also keeps her husband Chuck on his toes by requesting new shaped looms to add to their ever growing collection.

www.ingramcontent.com/pod-product-compliance
Lightning Source LLC
Chambersburg PA
CBHW061452050726
47593CB00004B/1565